Wanderlust

How to travel —

GUILT FREE

Essential tips for ethical travellers

Published in 2021 by Welbeck
An imprint of the Welbeck Publishing Group
20 Mortimer Street
London W1T 3JW

Copyright © 2021 Wanderlust Publications
Text written by Hazel Plush

A CIP catalogue for this book is available from the British Library.

ISBN 978-1-78739-615-9

Printed in China

10 9 8 7 6 5 4 3 2 1

The publishers would like to thank the following sources for their kind permission to
reproduce the pictures in this book.

Anna Leskinen/Shutterstock: 4-5, 20, 33, 46, 56, 68, 90, 114

Every effort has been made to acknowledge correctly and contact the source and/or
copyright holder of each picture and Welbeck Publishing apologises for any unintentional
errors or omissions, which will be corrected in future editions of this book.

Wanderlust

— *How to travel* —
GUILT FREE
Essential tips for ethical travellers

WELBECK

Contents

Introduction

Can you really have an amazing holiday that doesn't cost the Earth? Travel takes the rap for a long list of crimes: environmental crises, global warming, the spread of diseases and as a travel-lover you can feel like these issues are pinned to you too. You're told to fly less, stop exploring, to feel guilty about the trips you enjoy. But is staying at home really the answer?

Of course not. Instead, it's all about improving the way we travel. The places we choose to explore, the methods we use to get there, the attitude that we bring, and how lightly we tread. Travel is a force for good: it enriches life, provides livelihoods, and casts a fatal blow to prejudice. In the fight to save endangered wildlife and fragile landscapes, the tourism dollar is one of the world's greatest weapons; and it protects people, too – those who are under threat, on the edge of society, or simply trying to support their family.

If you stopped travelling, none of this would be possible.

But that doesn't mean we can't all do better – and you probably agree, as you're reading this book. It's not a compendium of Dos and Don'ts: it's a practical guide to making your holidays more sustainable, and is packed with advice for all parts of your trip. Should you carbon-offset your flights? What makes a home-stay so special? You'll learn about the nifty travel gear being made from landfill plastic; how tourism can empower whole communities; the shocking truth behind jet-skiing, dune-bashing and more – as well as the incredible alternatives to try instead.

Being a responsible traveller, you see, doesn't just make your trip "greener": it makes it more fun, more rewarding, and leads the way for others to do the same. Follow these tips, and you'll experience things that will alter your outlook forever, and cross paths with people that will change your life. For too long, travel has been seen as the problem – but in fact, it's the solution. So, don't stop adventuring: just do it better. Here's how…

HAZEL PLUSH, *WANDERLUST*

Chapter 1
PLANNING YOUR TRIP

Whether it's a mini-break, a sun-seeking getaway, or a globetrotting adventure – every holiday has the power to change the world for good. Being a better traveller is easier (and cheaper) than you might think. These tips will set you on the right path – from picking a destination to packing your bags...

1 *Pick an eco-friendly destination*

When it comes to sustainability, different countries have different priorities. So if responsible travel really is important to you, take a look at your destination's eco-credentials before you book. Are its nature reserves outstanding? What's its stance on single-use plastic? Does it provide an amazing experience without short-changing the environment?

Find a place whose priorities align with yours. France, for example, was the first country in the world to announce a total ban on the sale of single-use plastic cups, cutlery, plates and takeout boxes. Meanwhile, in Costa Rica, 90 per cent of the country's energy supply is renewable – thanks to its abundant geothermal, wind and hydroelectric resources. It aims to become entirely carbon-neutral by 2050.

WOULD YOU TAKE THE PLEDGE?

On arrival in Palau, Micronesia, your passport will be stamped with a promise: to "tread lightly, act kindly and explore mindfully" – which you, in turn, must sign. Do you think that's a step too far, or a worthwhile way to get visitors to commit to conservation?

Don't stick to *high* season

High season means high prices, but that's just one con of travelling at peak time. There are more crowds, more strain on resources, and – in overtourism pinch points like Venice and Paris – more tension between locals and visitors. If you stay out of season, you might sacrifice a few sunny days, but you'll find your destination much calmer, cheaper and quieter.

Here are some low-season surprises:

- The Maldives in October and November – the rain clouds are clearing, but prices haven't crept up yet. A great time to grab a bargain.

- Porto, Portugal, in March and April – you'll find a city that's in full spring swing before the summer hordes arrive.

- Langkawi, Malaysia, in September and October – days are hot, but afternoons bring short tropical showers while you snooze in a hammock.

3 *Book with the experts*

Before you book your trip, quiz your tour operator or travel agent:

- What's their policy on environmental issues, such as single-use plastic and carbon offsetting?

- Do they support any charities? If so, what proportion of their profits are donated?

- How do they ensure any wildlife experiences are sustainable?

A good travel company will have a strong stance on all of the above, and even go beyond expectations – by providing its customers with reusable water bottles, for example, or working closely with community outreach projects.

They should be able to provide you with solid proof of their efforts, too, such as fundraising figures or industry accreditation. It's easy to be dazzled by incredible itineraries, great reviews and amazing photography – but think of your booking as an investment. You're not only securing a great holiday for yourself but ensuring that the people and places you visit will be looked after too. If you spend your money wisely, everybody wins.

4 *Do your **research***

Those unplanned, impromptu travel experiences can be the stuff of magic – but it also pays to plan in advance because...

- **Not everything is as it seems**
  Is that wildlife sanctuary *really* as good as it sounds? Read the reviews, check the critics – and make an informed decision.

- **You can find the best route**
  The most obvious one isn't always the most responsible. Is a domestic flight really necessary – or can you find a lower-carbon alternative?

- **It's less faff while you're away**
  You won't be tied to the Wi-Fi, researching your next hotel/ activity/destination – and missing out on the here and now.

5
*Take fewer trips — but **stay longer***

While it's tempting to pack your weekends with minibreaks, keep those shorter trips close to home – and save up your annual leave for one big adventure. Not only will you minimize your carbon footprint, but you'll have much longer to get under the skin of the country and enjoy lots more time to unwind.

6

Volunteer for **conservation** *projects*

Could you squeeze a few days of volunteering into your break?
You don't have to dedicate months to make a difference:
some wildlife projects and conservation charities appreciate casual
helpers too.

Unfortunately, some schemes don't live up to their promises:
they're money-making enterprises rather than forces for good, so it's
vital to find – and rigorously research – any charities or placements
before you travel. Beware those that charge big fees (though a daily
donation is commonplace) or promise hands-on action – such as
feeding, administering treatments or playing with animals. Those
activities should be done by qualified vets, not untrained travellers.

At a responsible wildlife volunteering placement, your duties might
include mucking out or chopping up food for the animals. It's not
glamorous, but it's so rewarding to be involved.

7

Be *picky* about your hotel...

Where possible, always opt for an eco-conscious hotel or hostel: check its website to see if there's a green mission statement and take a look at online reviews. Also, widen your search on sustainability-focused accommodation directories, such as bookdifferent.com – which is recommended by the Global Sustainable Tourism Council. Its hotel partners must meet strict credentials, such as committing to recycling, reducing energy consumption and working closely with local communities.

And don't limit yourself to comparison websites – consult guidebooks, blogs and travel magazines too.

TOP TIP:

Beware of "greenwashing", in which companies claim their actions are more eco-friendly than they really are. Your best defence? Research.

8 *...or make yourself at **home***

What about a homestay? By staying with a family, you'll fit right into local life – with insider advice on where to go, what to eat and how to get around. It's usually far cheaper than other accommodation options, but your money can change the lives of your hosts.

While there are homestays all over the world (check out homestay.com and homestayin.com, as well as airbnb), local directories are often the best-connected – such as casaparticularcuba.org in Cuba and lookafterme.co.nz in New Zealand. See if there's one in your destination, too.

9 *Is there an **eco** lodge?*

In wilder locations, look out for eco lodges – they're designed to get you close (but not too close!) to the flora and fauna that make it so special, while also protecting them too. Located everywhere from the Amazon rainforest to Australia's national parks, these sustainable dwellings tread lightly on the land – using solar energy, rainwater collecting, permaculture farming and much more. Many also work with local charities and communities to ensure that they benefit from tourism.

There are thousands of eco lodges all over the world, but for a good benchmark of what to aim for check out Rewa Eco-Lodge in Guyana (rewaecolodge.com), Bambu Indah in Indonesia (bambuindah.com) and Ecuador's Mashpi Lodge (mashpilodge.com). Also, look for local or national accreditations, such as Costa Rica's Certification for Sustainable Tourism (govisitcostarica.com) and The Rainforest Alliance's Green Vacations in the Caribbean and Latin America (rainforest-alliance.org/green-vacations).

10 *Choose the* *right* rental

In some destinations, rental properties have fallen from favour – and with good reason. Where accommodation demand is high, holiday lettings can drive up house prices for locals, put a strain on the economy and play into the hands of profit-grabbing landlords.

To combat this, they're closely regulated by authorities. In Mallorca, for example, airbnb hosts must have an official registration number – while in New York City short-term lets are mostly illegal. So, before you book, double-check that your hosts are above board: if they're not, it could be a scam or you might be fined.

And beware of any suspiciously cheap rentals: if it sounds too good to be true, it probably is.

11

Where to wash?

On longer trips, laundry can be a huge expense. But instead of shelling out for a hotel service, take your dirties to a local laundrette. You'll find them in residential areas, away from tourist hotspots – which is a great excuse to explore a new place... Just got a few things to wash? Pop them in the base of your shower to make maximum use of your suds. A biodegradable detergent will help too: try Sea To Summit's Liquid Laundry Wash (seatosummit.co.uk). Also, the abrasive interior of Scrubba's mini washing bag (thescrubba.com) makes hand-laundry easy – lending plenty of extra oomph!

12 *Rethink* *DEET*

DEET (or, as it's officially known, N,N-Diethyl-meta-toluamide) is a chemical insect repellent, found in various bug sprays and roll-ons. While it's great at deterring mosquitos, it is also highly toxic to fish and other animals – including dogs and cats. As such, some countries (such as Canada and the Netherlands) restrict the use of high-concentration DEET products.

So, should you ditch it? That depends on where you're travelling. If it's somewhere with lots of mosquito-borne diseases, ask your doctor for advice. However, on most holidays, DEET could be swapped for something more eco-friendly – such as Incognito's 100 per cent natural sprays (lessmosquito.com) or a botanical-based product from No Mozzie (nomozzie.com). However, some plant-derived ingredients can be harmful to animals too (citronella is toxic to dogs, for example), so check with a travel clinic if you plan to mix with animals on your trip.

Source: National Pesticide Information Center (2008).

13 *Luggage that **treads** lightly*

Upgrading your suitcase? These stylish, hard-wearing bags benefit the environment too...

- **The suitcase**
  Spark SNG ECO Spinner Suitcase, Samsonite
  With fabric made from plastic bottles, and trimmed with responsibly sourced cork, Samsonite's ECO four-wheeler is a winner: samsonite.co.uk

- **The duffel bag**
  Black Hole 70l Duffel Bag, Patagonia
  Stuff your gear into a hard-wearing, adventure-ready holdall – made with 100 per cent recycled body fabric, lining and webbing: patagonia.com

- **The day bag**
  The Jett Bag, Seahorse Bags
  You'd never guess that Seahorse's nifty backpacks – big enough to fit a day's essentials – are made from 38 plastic bottles. Ten per cent of profits go to an ocean clean-up charity, too: seahorsebags.com

14 *Pack **savvy***

The lighter you travel, the easier it is to explore. You can nip between buses, bypass queues in airports, and arrive far quicker (and happier) than those who haul a huge suitcase around.

If you'll be relying on drivers or porters for help with your luggage, it's only fair to lighten the load. And, whether you're travelling by rickshaw or jumbo jet, a smaller bag means lower fuel consumption. It's great news for the environment – and your back will thank you, too.

15 *Bring a bottle*
– and use it

Investing in a reusable water bottle is an easy first step to ditching single-use plastic for good: look to Camelbak (camelbak.com) or Nalgene (nalgene.com) for lightweight and durable BPA-free bottles. They're hard-wearing and built to withstand both expedition conditions and regular use, but if a component does break – or you lose a lid, for example – most manufacturers supply spare parts too. It'll save you some cash and give the bottle a much longer life.

WHEN THE TAP ISN'T TIP-TOP

If water quality is a worry in your destination, try a self-filtering Water-to-Go bottle (watertogo.eu): its filters remove 99.9 per cent of microbiological contaminants, so you can fill up from any non-saltwater source – even a murky stream or dodgy-looking tap. You'll need to replace the filter every few months (or 200 litres/ 44 gallons), but they're suitable for household recycling.

16 *Pack your own body wash...*

... and make it a biodegradable one. While it's always a good idea to opt for an all-natural, eco-friendly product, it's especially pertinent if you're heading to a destination where waste water treatment isn't as rigorous as it is at home. Your shower run-off could be discarded into water sources or used to irrigate crops – with those chemically derived suds tainting the environment and aquatic food chain.

Opt for a biodegradable body wash – such as Faith in Nature's British-made hard soaps (faithinnature.co.uk) – for a lather that'll break down quickly and organically. Another benefit of hard soaps: you can slice some off to keep in your day bag (in a soap box or sealable sandwich bag) for eco-friendly handwashing on the go.

17 *Use reef-safe* **sunscreen**

Sea-swimmers and snorkellers take note: regular suncreams contain oxybenzone and octinoxate, which wreak havoc on marine life. The moment you slip into the water, they do too – polluting the ecosystem and even contributing to coral bleaching. And of course, your skin isn't protected if it's not slathered up so you'll risk sunburn and heatstroke, while also choking the reef.

Palau, Hawaii and Florida's Key West have already pledged to banish chemical-based sunscreens, asking visitors to use mineral-based, reef-safe cream instead. It sits on the skin (rather than being absorbed), blocking UV rays with zinc oxide and titanium dioxide. Even if you're staying on dry land, it's worth checking out: oxybenzone and octinoxate have also been linked to increased cancer risk and fertility problems.

SAVVY SUN CARE

For the best sun protection while you're swimming, invest in a UV-rated rash vest: the lightweight, quick-drying material can block up to 98 per cent of the sun's rays. Look for the Skin Cancer Foundation's Seal of Recommendation (skincancer.org).

18 *Choose kit with a **conscience***

- **Travel towels**
  Quick-drying, sand-repellent and colourful. Check out Dock & Bay's beach towels, made from made entirely from recycled plastic bottles: dockandbay.com

- **Picnic mats**
  The only kind of plastic you should ever throw on the ground. Life Under Canvas transforms old plastic straws into eye-catching picnic mats: lifeundercanvas.co.uk

- **Tents**
  Made from 69 plastic bottles, Vango's Devon 300 tent is lightweight, hard-wearing, and can be pitched in just 10 minutes. Ideal for hikers: vango.co.uk

- **Packing cubes**
  They'll keep your suitcase organized, and your conscience clean. Vespula's packing cubes are made from recycled polyester: vespulaluggage.co.uk

- **Passport holders**
  Dumela Crafts turns landfill waste into stylish passport holders – while supporting artisans and communities throughout South Africa: dumelacrafts.com

19
Are you covered?

Only fools travel without insurance. While it's not the most thrilling of purchases, the right cover will protect you – and your wallet – if accident, illness or disruption strike.

And it doesn't only benefit you. Policies that include premium healthcare and heli-evacuation, for example, also help to ease strain on remote or underfunded facilities. How reliable is the medical system in your destination? How far-flung will you be? In instances of widespread illness or disruption, robust travel insurance is priceless.

20 *Eco-proof your **home***

There's no use planning an eco-friendly holiday if your house is still guzzling energy. Before you leave, don't forget to:

- Unplug all your electronics, especially those on standby

- Turn down the thermostat – or put it on "eco" mode

- Pause deliveries of your newspapers or magazines

- Close all doors and windows to keep the heat in or out

- Find the stop tap – and turn it off to prevent leaks

Chapter 2

GETTING THERE AND AROUND

Travel has never been more eco-conscious. With investment in biofuels, efficiency and green technology, transport is treading increasingly lightly – but it still has a long way to go. So, what's the best way to cover some ground? Here's how to lessen your carbon footprint while exploring further than ever before...

21 *Make the journey count*

Any form of motor-powered travelling – whether by plane, scooter, train or boat – has an environmental toll. Indeed, transportation accounts for around a quarter of the world's human-induced carbon footprint: road vehicles are the biggest polluter (they account for 74 per cent of transportation emissions), followed by domestic and international flights (12 per cent).

But, as you'll discover throughout this chapter, there are myriad ways to minimize your emissions. The first? Prioritize low-impact choices and make them part of the adventure – a challenge, yes, but it'll soon become second nature. For starters, try these ideas:

- Taking a long-distance train instead of short flights (see seat61.com for route ideas)

- Swapping taxis for lift-shares and carpooling (try blablacar.com or liftshare.com)

- Embracing your own power! Squeeze as much walking and cycling into your holiday
  Source: Air Transport Action Group, 2020

22

*Stay **flexible***

Getting from A to B isn't only a carbon concern. Sometimes, despite your best intentions, a journey could be unwise for other reasons: because of local lockdowns perhaps, or risky situations such as wildfires, flooding or unstable terrain. Rather than forcing your way through, and potentially putting yourself (and others) in harm's way, try to be as flexible as you can. For added peace of mind, make a back-up plan and book refundable hotels or activities.

23 *Ride the* **rails**

The world's rail systems have never been better connected or more energy efficient – and those aren't the only perks. Choose trains, and not only will you travel more mindfully, but you'll get to know the country – and its people – far better. From subways to sleepers, each ride adds to your story: you'll learn as you go, picking up the local language, travel tips and much more.

And of course, it's usually a much greener option than flying or driving. Operators are electrifying lines and replacing diesel trains with quieter, cleaner locomotives – and many European ones run on hydroelectric or wind-powered energy. Northern Germany is home to the world's first hydrogen-powered passenger train, the Coradia iLint, whose only waste product is water. Now that's an idea you can get on board with.

24 *Pick the right flight*

With developments in biofuels, energy efficiency and waste disposal, flying is becoming more sustainable than ever – but it still has a huge environmental impact. In the UK alone, aviation accounts for 6 per cent of the nation's greenhouse gas emissions – while globally it's responsible for around 2 per cent of all human-induced CO_2. If you must fly, make sure you...

Go direct
Taking off and landing use more fuel than cruising, so book a non-stop flight if you can.

Book wisely
Spend your money with an airline that strives for sustainability – with innovation, recycling and charity support.

Keep it low
Emissions vary widely between aircraft types. Skyscanner's Greener Choice search function is a handy tool: skyscanner.net
Sources: Air Transport Action Group, 2020; Committee on Climate Change

25 *Should you* **carbon** *offset?*

Offsetting enables you to counteract your carbon-negative choices by investing in carbon-positive schemes. Many different companies, including some airlines, offer this service: based on your carbon emissions, they'll calculate a donation – which is then invested in renewable energy technology or reforestation projects, for example.

However, it's not always black and white (or green): some critics claim that carbon offsetting encourages unsustainable behaviour – a "permission to pollute". We should be embracing good habits, they say, instead of paying to keep bad ones.

But whatever your view, flying and offsetting is always better than flying and *not* offsetting.

WHAT'S THE REAL PRICE?
A return flight from London Heathrow to New York's JFK Airport produces roughly 2,863 kg (6,312 lb) of carbon dioxide per passenger – that's more than the average car pumps out per year. To offset it, you'd need to pay around £60.
Source: atmosfair.de, August 2020

26

Take your inflight essentials

On average, airline passengers generate more than 5.7 million tonnes of cabin waste per year, says the International Air Transport Association – so how can we put a dent in that? Carbon offsetting isn't enough. Say no to the plastic-wrapped blankets provided on planes (bring your own instead) and ask the crew to fill up your water bottle instead of using disposable cups.

Give back those in-flight amenity kits and invest in some decent essentials instead: a good pair of flight socks, eye shades and headphones will last you for years.

Also, find out how your airline processes plastic waste. Some are doing their bit: Air New Zealand has banished some single-use plastic items from its flights, Cathay Pacific and Qantas are pioneering biofuels, and charter carrier Hi Fly launched the world's first single-use plastic-free flights last year. Change is coming – at last.

27

*What about the **ferry**?*

Some ferry companies are leading the way for sustainable sea-travel – by committing to biofuels, embracing low-emission technologies, and supporting marine conservation projects. Hop on board...

- Boreal Sjø (Norway) is introducing two zero-emission vessels. The battery-powered ships will enter circulation in 2021: boreal.no

- Fred Olsen Express (throughout the Canary Islands, Spain) works with local charities and researchers to protect marine life: fredolsen.es

- Stena Line (throughout Europe) converts on-board food waste into biogas on some vessels: stenaline.co.uk

28 *Cruise with a conscience*

Cruise ships have a bad reputation, but it's not always deserved. Some operators, alas, do little to lessen their environmental toll, happy to chug through the oceans at the cost of fragile ecosystems and island communities – however, habits are changing. For example, the Cruise Lines International Association (CLIA; cruising. org) ensures that its members (including Cunard, Royal Caribbean and MSC) stick to a strict Environmental Protection policy, with adherence to responsible waste management, energy consumption and more.

Others are showing an even deeper commitment: such as Hurtigruten (hurtigruten.co.uk), whose *MS Roald Amundsen* is the world's first hybrid, battery-supported cruise ship – and Ecoventura (ecoventura.com), which has won awards for its small-group, low-carbon sailings through Ecuador's Galápagos Islands.

DID YOU KNOW?
The cruise industry recycles 60 per cent more waste per person than the average person does on land in the USA.
Source: CLIA

Responsible on the river

Rivers are often the lifeblood of a destination: they splice some of the world's most exciting cities, and connect to far-flung places unreachable by road. Cruising them, then, allows for vibrant itineraries through the heart of a country – whether you follow the Danube across Europe, or the Mississippi through America's Deep South. These responsible river cruise companies are making waves...

- The *Victoria Mekong*, operated by Wendy Wu Tours, uses solar power, low-energy cruising speeds and is committed to becoming 100 per cent plastic free: wendywutours.co.uk

- Uniworld partners with conservation charities and projects to protect the world's waterways – and champions authentic, family-run activities on its trips: uniworld.com

- Avalon Waterways strives to reduce its carbon footprint by cutting down on everything from plastic laundry bags to paper brochures: avalonwaterways.co.uk

PADDLE POWER

A river kayaking or SUP trip can give you a fresh perspective on a city you thought you knew. From the water, even the most famous metropolis looks different: just try NYC's Manhattan Kayak rentals (manhattankayak.com), or night-paddling through London with Secret Adventures (secretadventures.org).

30 *Embrace electric*

All the big car rental companies now offer EVs (electric vehicles) – including Avis, Hertz and Sixt. Of course, some destinations are better equipped than others, but charging stations are on the rise globally – and websites like chargemap.com will help you find them.

Accommodation providers, too, are installing power-points: Charge Hotels (chargehotels.com) lists almost 6,000 electric-friendly properties, while Marriott has installed more than 3,000 points at its hotels all over the world.

EVs are revolutionizing the safari experience, too. In Botswana, Chobe Game Lodge offers electric boats and vehicles for watching elephants along the Chobe River (chobegamelodge.com). South Africa's Cheetah Plains, meanwhile, has four electric Land Cruisers: all the better for witnessing its namesake big cats (cheetahplains.com).

31
Go public

While public transport isn't always a low-emission way of
getting around, sharing a ride is a better option than going it
alone. And of course, whether you're on a bus in Uzbekistan
or a *tro tro* in Ghana, public transport lets you rub shoulders
with the people who call the place home: giving you a
more immersive, authentic experience.

32 *Try pedal power*

On city breaks, swap the subway for a rental bike: they're cheaper, greener, and mean you can definitely order dessert…

THREE OF THE BEST BIKE-FRIENDLY CITIES

Copenhagen, Denmark

With almost 400 km (250 miles) of dedicated bike lanes and cycle superhighways connecting it to other destinations, Denmark's capital sets the bar in Europe. The official bike rental scheme is Bycyklen (bycyklen.dk).

Montréal, Canada

There are over 6,000 BIXI bikes for rental throughout Montréal – available from 610 stations across the city (bixi.com). Generous investment has created 700 km (435 miles) of cycle lanes, and there's even a bike festival too.

Portland, USA

The BIKETOWN cycle-sharing scheme keeps Portland, Oregon moving (biketownpdx.com). There are 1,000 bikes for hire, as well as adaptive models for riders with disabilities. Look out for free maps and rental lockers.

33

*On **two** feet...*

On a good walk, everyone wins. It's great for the environment, as well as the body and mind – and you'll forge a deeper connection to local life. You don't have to embark on a long-distance hike to feel the benefits: how about an art-themed walking tour of a city, or an on-foot safari experience?

34

...or two wheels

You can cover more ground, keep fit while you travel and get a front-row view wherever you venture – what's not to love about cycling? Whether by road bike, push bike or e-bike (a powered model that makes mountains a breeze), exploring on two wheels is endlessly rewarding – and with the rise of cycling holidays and official sightseeing routes, it's becoming increasingly accessible, too.

Love mountain biking? Try bikepacking, which combines trail runs with wild camping – for a buzz that lasts for as long as your legs can carry you. You'll find tips and tricks at bikepacking.com.

35
Don't print your ticket

The days of having to print out your boarding pass, hotel reservation and insurance docs are over. Hurrah! Not only is your bag a lot lighter, but the environmental impact is too. However, don't just store them on your phone: email them to yourself too – so if you lose your phone or get into trouble, they're easy to access or send to someone who can help.

36 *Smaller is better*

When it comes to tour groups, smaller is always better. Not only will your experience be more personalized and immersive, but you'll tread much more lightly too. Travelling in coachloads means whistle-stop tours, sticking to the main drag, and missing that extra-special restaurant/viewpoint/attraction. That's not what you want on your holiday, is it? Some small-group specialists:

- Responsible Travel – whose Trip for a Trip initiative also supports disadvantaged young people: responsibletravel.com

- Exodus Travel – for adventure holidays and cultural breaks with local guides: exodus.co.uk

- Wild Frontiers – taking intrepid travellers to little-visited destinations: wildfrontierstravel.com

37

If you're camping, keep it clean

Some people seem to think that the countryside has its own team of cleaners – poised to scoop up their rubbish bags and disposable BBQs as soon as they leave. The scorched earth from their campfire will magically heal, and their toilet paper (and worse) will vanish from hedgerows. This, of course, is not the case.

If you're staying in a campsite, it'll likely have its own rules – so stick to them. If you're wild camping, the following should always apply:

- Check local laws. Is wild camping legal there? Do you need the landowner's permission?
- Arrive late and leave early. Get there at dusk, and be gone by the time day-trippers return.
- Never light an open fire. The environmental hazards are huge.
- Leave no trace. When you move on, the site should be exactly as you found it – no excuses.
- Be considerate. Keep away from main pathways and tracks. If you're asked to leave, do so.

38 *Keep mileage to a **minimum***

Covering a lot of ground? Check into different hotels as you go – rather than slogging back to the same one every night. The environmental benefits are obvious, but you'll also support lots of local businesses and enjoy more time to explore. Chances are, the regular tour groups and day-trippers will be gone by late afternoon, leaving you with the place almost all to yourself.

39

Are you going my way?

Lift sharing or carpooling isn't just an environmentally friendly choice – it makes sense for your budget, too. While some websites connect travellers with drivers (blablacar.com and liftshare.com are good places to start), make some in-person enquiries as well: leave a note on your hostel messageboard, or ask the hotel receptionist if they know anyone heading your way. If the plan works, pay it forward: if your driver covers the petrol, perhaps you could buy their entrance tickets or lunch? Always make sure to inform trusted people where you're going and who you are with.

40 *Take the road less **travelled***

Sometimes, a place can be too popular for its own good – just look at Barcelona's heaving Las Ramblas and the rubbish-choked trail to Everest's summit. Overtourism doesn't only steal the magic of a place – it also decimates ecosystems, disrupts economies and makes local life a nightmare too.

The answer? Slip away to somewhere under-the-radar instead:

- 120 million tourists visit the Swiss and Austrian Alps every year – but Slovenia's Julian Alps are spectacular, crowd-free and ripe for exploring.

- Amsterdam attracts almost 20 million city-breakers annually – while little-visited Rotterdam (an hour away) offers waterside gastronomy and art galleries galore.

- Seville is crazy in summer – and the rest of the year, too. But what about Jerez de la Frontera (only 75 minutes south by train) for Flamenco, tapas and wine tasting?

Chapter 3
DURING YOUR STAY

Think of it as a challenge: what can you do on your trip to leave a positive impact? It could be something small, like trying a community-run cooking class, or something much bigger, such as hiring a local guide for the day. Make it fun and engaging, and remember it needn't be hard work: this is a holiday, after all!

41

Don't leave your good ***habits*** *at home*

Recycling, reusing, respecting other people… all those great things
that you do in your daily life are just as important on holiday. Isn't it
strange how some people forget to pack their morals and manners
when they go away? Don't be one of them!

42 *Make health a priority*

If 2020 taught us one thing, it's that health should always come first. So, do your research:

- What's the likelihood of local lockdowns? Are there any places that aren't welcoming visitors?

- Will you need a mask or face covering? If so, where? Are there any other requirements?

- What's the local policy on COVID testing? Should you factor in extra flexibility to your itinerary?

43

Know your own mind

If something doesn't look or feel right, trust your gut. It's easy to go along with the crowd – but don't compromise your own beliefs to avoid causing a fuss. There's no shame in retreating from the situation with your principles intact. It can take nerve, especially if you're with people who don't share your misgivings – but isn't it better to have a few awkward moments than a lifetime of regret?

44 *What's the etiquette?*

Behaviour that's perfectly polite in one destination could be downright rude in another. You might be surprised...

* Burping at the dinner table is a compliment in China: it shows that you enjoyed the meal greatly.

* Slurping noodles is encouraged in Japan: it supposedly improves the flavours and makes hot dishes easier to eat.

* Clinking beer glasses to say cheers is rude in Hungary, but it's fine for wine or *pálinka* (fruit brandy).

45 *Clean up your act*

Look out for meetups with like-minded people where you're travelling – they'll add a whole new dimension to your trip. Joining an organized litter-pick, for example, can be a rewarding way to give back, and there's often a strong social scene too. Throughout Asia and Europe, environmental network Trash Hero (trashhero. org) coordinates regular garbage-gathering events: since it was founded in 2013, its volunteers have cleared over 1 million kilos (22 million pounds) of the stuff. The 2019 Great British Beach Clean collected 10,800 kg (23,800 lb) of trash from Britain's shores in just one weekend (mcsuk.org). Let's work to keep that momentum going.

46 *Leave* no *trace*

Caught short in the great outdoors? Wild wees are fine, though make sure you're at least 200 m/650 ft (preferably further) from the nearest water source. The same rule applies for number twos, which you should bury – not under a rock, but in the earth (15–20 cm/6–8 in deep). When camping, take a trowel to dig a hole. Sea to Summit's pocket-size option folds down to a discreet size and weighs just 87 g (3 oz): seatosummit.co.uk

And it should go without saying: take all of your used toilet paper with you. Pop it in a good-quality ziplock bag, then dispose of it safely.

47 *Dress for the occasion*

You might not want to cover your head or swap your shorts for trousers – but you don't make the rules. It's a sign of respect to follow the local dress code, regardless of whether you agree with it or not. If you don't, you might be refused entry to places, attract unwanted attention or get into trouble with the authorities.

TOP TIP:

When visiting sensitive areas or places of worship, savvy travellers always pack a lightweight (but opaque) cover-up. In some temples, you'll need to remove your footwear: if you're wearing sandals, bring a pair of socks to avoid having to go barefoot.

48 *Address the legacy*

Travel can be the best history lesson – but it doesn't always sit comfortably. A guidebook might wax lyrical about a city's "colonial charm", yet not address the bloody regime that once ruled it. You might stay in a picturesque sugar plantation, or in a sumptuous palace that was built by imperialists – but leave none the wiser about its cruel origins. Often, there's a tacit *don't ask, don't tell* undercurrent: your hosts probably don't want to dwell on the past, while you feel too uncomfortable to question it. Nobody should have to apologize for atrocities they didn't commit – but if we don't talk about it, aren't we just reinforcing that colonial gaze?

So make it your mission to be as informed as possible, to research the history (both good and bad) of your destination – and, where possible, seek out places that don't airbrush the truth. Ask questions, garner opinions, be interested: only then can we really learn from the past.

49

*Tribal tourism – **good** or **bad?***

At best, tourism can empower indigenous communities – but at worst, these encounters are akin to a human zoo. "In principle, there is little harm in tourists visiting tribal peoples who have been in routine contact with outsiders for some time," says Survival International, which campaigns on behalf of indigenous peoples all over the world. "But this only applies to tribal peoples who are happy to receive visitors, have proper control over where the tourists go and what they do in their communities, and receive a fair share of the profits."

Do your research before you book – and if travelling with a tour operator, quiz them about their safeguarding protocols. Be mindful of health, too: for close-contact visits, there's the risk of you introducing unfamiliar illnesses. Are you fighting fit, or might you be carrying an ailment that could spread through a remote community?

50

Approach slum tours cautiously

In many cities where deprivation is rife, slum tours are marketed as a way to raise awareness and boost the economy – but you should choose your experience carefully. Look for companies with good reviews, no-camera policies, and proven initiatives to support the local community.

- In Mumbai, Reality Tours & Travel takes travellers into the Dharavi slum – to meet its talented artisans and join a cooking class with a local family. It channels 80 per cent of profits back into the community: realitytoursandtravel.com

- In Rio de Janeiro, tour guide Marcelo Armstrong hosts engaging, enlightening walks through the Rocinha favela – the largest one in Brazil – with proceeds supporting local education programmes: favelatour.com.br

51 *Champion local know-how*

Using local guides can turn a holiday into the adventure of a lifetime – and make a real positive economic impact on your destination. Aside from the obvious advantages of travelling with someone who *really* knows the area, local guides have a wealth of knowledge and a vested interest in giving you an outstanding, authentic experience. Many have a topic they specialize in too, such as wildlife or photography – so choose one whose expertise aligns with your interests.

If you're travelling with a tour operator, ask them how they recruit guides – and whether they offer them training, insurance and high-quality equipment (which they should). Also, check out the Wanderlust World Guide Awards (worldguideawards.com) to see some of the best ones in the business.

52
Bring a gift

If you've booked a homestay or a tour with a local guide, consider bringing a "thank you" gift from home. To you, it might just be a simple box of shortbread or packet of tea – but to your host, it could be a taste of a place they've always dreamed of visiting. If you forget, or if suitcase space is at a premium, try to seek out a local delicacy instead.

Note: a gift should never be in lieu of a tip.

53 *Seek out the unexpected*

It might be a street-art tour of Mexico City, a supper club evening in San Francisco or a farmstay in rural New Zealand: wherever you go, try at least one experience that strives to be unique. Not only will you get a glimpse of local life beyond the must-sees, but these attractions and activities are often run by passionate, pioneering entrepreneurs. Look out for recommendations in blogs and on social media – and use these sites as a starting point:

- airbnb's quirky Experiences include a DJ masterclass in Cuba, sandboarding in Oman, horse-whispering in Spain – and that's just the start: airbnb.co.uk/experiences

- Make My Day puts travellers in touch with expert local guides throughout Europe – for kayaking trips, gin-tasting and even a penny-farthing tour of London: makemyday.travel

- Viatour has lots of intriguing experiences – like gelato-tasting in Florence, a line-dancing class in Nashville and behind-the-scenes Bollywood tours: viator.com

- Backstreet Academy matches travellers with artisans throughout Southeast Asia – for masterclasses in calligraphy, art, cooking and more: backstreetacademy.com

54

Keep it community-focused

When you put a community in charge of a travel company or eco lodge, amazing things can happen. Take Il Ngwesi, a safari camp in Kenya, which is owned and run by the Masai tribe: not only does it provide incredible wildlife encounters, but guests get to learn about this rich culture too, with its remarkable hunting techniques and vibrant music and dancing (ilngwesi.com). In Ecuador's Yasuni National Park, Sani Lodge – a rainforest hideaway – is owned by the indigenous Kichwa people, and profits are channelled straight back into local education (sanilodge.com). And in Western Australia, the Kooljaman wilderness camp enables the Bardi Jawi people to share their 40,000 years of history with visitors from all over the world (kooljaman.com.au).

Once you've stayed in one community-owned lodge, and seen the great work they can do, you'll want to seek them out wherever you travel.

55

Be bossy in the bathroom

You know the drill: leave your towel hanging up if you want to reuse it, or put it on the floor if you need a fresh one. But some hotel housekeeping teams don't seem to get the message – or are told to ignore it. If raising your frustration with management doesn't do the job (maybe remind them that saving water also saves them money), some travellers resort to more wily means: for example, hiding towels in wardrobes so they don't join the laundry pile, bringing their own ones instead, or displaying the Do Not Disturb sign whenever they leave the room.

56 *Eat **local***

Make a beeline for independently owned restaurants, and always opt for locally sourced dishes rather than imported fare: the fewer food miles, the better. It might be tempting to stick to global restaurant chains that you're familiar with, but eating local ensures that your cash goes to the people who need it most – and the environment benefits too. Plus, you'll never make any amazing food discoveries by playing it safe...

57 *Find a **fixer***

Broken the zip on your suitcase? Worn a hole in your shoes?
Sometimes, travel gear falters at the most inconvenient time – but
rather than binning it, is there someone nearby who could repair it?
Cobblers and tailors can bring even the most battered belongings
back to life – particularly in places where resources are scarce. Ask
around for recommendations, and always agree a fee in advance.

58 *Haggle **wisely***

In many countries, you'd be crazy not to haggle – it's part of the culture, and the only way to avoid getting ripped off. But in places where trade is quiet or tourists are scarce, that 10-dollar discount will have a far greater impact on the vendor than you, so ask yourself if it's worth it. We all love a bargain, but is there a moral cost too?

59 *Be **careful** where you buy*

You're visiting a craft workshop, browsing beautiful hand-painted ceramics and watching the artisans at work – but something doesn't seem right. Are those young craftsmen really apprentices, or are they kids being forced into labour? Do they have decent working conditions, or do they look hunched-over, exhausted or scared?

If the situation feels dodgy, don't part with your cash – even if a silver-tongued salesman assures you it's fine. Keep your eyes open and, if travelling on an organized tour, raise your concerns with your guide. If you're still not happy, chat to your tour operator: they have the power to force change or take their clients elsewhere.

60

*Do as the locals do – or **better***

Nobody's perfect – but even so, you might be dismayed by local behaviour while you're away. It might be a widespread reliance on plastic bags and single-use face coverings, or something less obvious, like a cultural festival that releases lanterns into the sky. Usually, it's in a traveller's interest to blend into their surroundings, to immerse themselves in the most authentic way – but if that doesn't feel good, then don't.

Instead, make a point of following your own compass – by asking where you can recycle your rubbish, for example, or shunning the zoo in favour of a guided wild hike. By setting an example, you'll show that visitors want more responsible experiences. Be the change that you want to see in the world.

Chapter 4
WHAT NOT TO DO

For all our good intentions, it's easy to be led astray – especially when exploring somewhere new. You might be hoodwinked into an activity you'd usually avoid, or find yourself unwittingly contributing to a problem. So, here's how to avoid such pitfalls – and some advice on things to do, say, or seek out instead…

61

*Don't... **burden** a donkey*

In destinations where the terrain is tough, it's not uncommon to see touts offering rides on donkeys and horses – but responsible travellers always give them a wide berth. If you'd struggle with Santorini's steep steps or Petra's uneven pathways, spare a thought for the exhausted mules that have to carry tourists up – and down – them all day.

And that's not the worst of it. "Many are poorly treated, neglected and beaten," says animal welfare charity SPANA, which campaigns for ethical equine tourism. "If you have animal welfare concerns on holiday, report them to the relevant country tourism board – and consult our Holiday Hooves Guide (spana.org) to find out how you can positively influence the treatment of animals overseas."

Only take part in mule- or horse-riding activities if they've been recommended by a responsible tour operator or animal welfare organization. And before you hop on, ensure your travel insurance includes it: in all likelihood, you'll need specialist cover.

62 *Don't... go dune-bashing*

Life in the desert is hard enough without 4WD vehicles "bashing" the dunes. Aside from the obvious noise and pollution, this white-knuckle ride disrupts the desert's fragile ecosystem, killing plants, scaring wildlife, and scattering the seeds that lie in the topmost sand waiting for rain. It's an environmental disaster, affecting every form of life in the desert – including the communities with deep economical and emotional ties to the land. Instead, try:

- A hot air balloon ride in Rajasthan, India, to watch the sunrise over the Thar Desert

- Camel riding through Morocco's Sahara Desert, with a starry night in a tented camp

- A safari through Dubai's Al Marmoom Desert Conservation Reserve, to spy Arabian oryx in the dunes

63 *Don't... miss the switch*

It's one of our biggest hotel bugbears: you turn everything off before leaving your room, but return to find the lights blazing, the ceiling fan whirling and even – for some unfathomable reason – the television playing to itself. It's time to have a quiet word with the hotel manager about housekeeping's aversion to off switches: they might not notice one complaint, but if we all say something perhaps the message will get through.

Tick off a mental checklist before you head out for the day: quiet energy-guzzlers such as air conditioning units, table lamps and water heaters are particularly easy to miss.

KEEP IT CLOSED!

According to research by the Carbon Trust (carbontrust.com), heating or air conditioning can account for up to 40 per cent of a hotel's energy bill – so if it's really hot or cold outside, make sure your windows are properly shut.

64

*Don't... be **reckless** on the reef*

Whether you're swimming, snorkelling or scuba diving, make sure you...

- Don't touch the marine life. Admire it, but don't grab it.

- Take care of the coral. Getting hands-on will hurt it – and maybe you too.

- Stay away from the bottom. Even just one fin-kick can damage it.

- Remember you're a guest. Leave the area as you found it.

- Take no souvenirs. Keep shells, rocks and coral where they belong.

65 Don't... "pet" lions

Lion petting is a sordid, sickening business. The opportunity to stroke, cuddle or walk with lions is depressingly common in southern Africa, where naive visitors pay for up-close encounters and photo opportunities. What they don't realize is that often those cubs have been snatched from their mothers, drugged and declawed, and can never be returned to the wild – no matter what their keepers claim.

When they're too big to manhandle, most of these lions are sold to zoos or "canned hunting" parks, where gun-toting tourists give small fortunes to kill them. Don't be fooled into supporting this hideous trade; instead, visit genuine sanctuaries such as South Africa's LIONSROCK (lionsrock.org) and Shamwari (shamwariconservationexperience.com) – where mistreated lions are given the care they deserve.

And of course, it's not only "petting" lions that are exploited for cash: many other big cats suffer a similar fate, in destinations all over the world.

66

Don't... visit orphanages

If presented with the opportunity to visit or volunteer in an orphanage, approach with extreme caution. "One of the biggest myths is that children in orphanages are there because they have no parents," advises welfare charity Save the Children. "This is not the case. Most are there because their parents simply can't afford to feed, clothe and educate them."

ReThink Orphanages, an international campaign group, offers further explanation: "In some cases, vulnerable families are targeted by corrupt orphanage owners who wish to 'recruit' children to fill the spaces in their orphanage and exploit them for financial gain."

This practice, known as orphanage trafficking, exists simply because well-meaning volunteers or visitors are so willing to part with their cash. The only answer is DON'T. Even if it seems like a bona-fide organization, ask yourself: why exactly are you being invited in?

67 *Don't... ride elephants*

Elephants are not entertainment. And yet, they are often forced to do circus tricks, paint with their trunks, kick balls – and carry humans on their backs. "Most 'domestic' elephants are wild-born, captured when young and trained using cruel techniques," says conservationist Ian Redmond OBE. "Watch any mahout manoeuvring an elephant through crowded streets and he'll likely be resting the point of his *ankus* (bull-hook) on its skin: a reminder that disobedience carries painful consequences."

The tourism dollar is the most powerful tool in the fight for animal welfare, so spend yours wisely: on safaris to see elephants in the wild, or bona-fide conservation efforts – such as Thailand's Elephant Nature Park (elephantnaturepark.org) and Elephant Hills tented camp (elephanthills.com).

A TRIUMPH TO TRUMPET

All responsible tour operators have ceased offering elephant rides: in 2014, Intrepid Travel (intrepidtravel.com) was the first major company to do so – but since then, hundreds of others have followed their lead. Bravo to that!

68

*Don't... make **unethical** food choices*

While trying new food is one of travel's great joys, beware of some delicacies. We're all too aware of the dangers that some unorthodox animal products present – especially the high risk of transmitting viruses across species. And of course, it's often an ethical minefield too.

In Africa, eating bushmeat endangers wildlife and has been linked to myriad diseases; in Asia, the likes of shark fin soup and turtle jelly make a grisly addition to many menus.

Indonesia's *kopi luwak* – "cat poo coffee" – might seem like a fun thing to try, but the civets are usually kept in cages and force-fed coffee beans to ensure a constant supply. The responsible verdict? Avoid.

OFF THE MENU?

Conch – a marine mollusc – is consumed in huge quantities throughout the Caribbean, but its numbers are threatened. The Bahamian government has even launched a "Conchservation" initiative, to help boost declining stocks – so you might want to think twice before ordering those famous conch fritters.

69

Don't... walk off **designated** *tracks*

Sometimes, when you're out hiking, it can be tempting to leave the trail. It might be the promise of a better view, the increased chance of seeing a rare bird, flower or butterfly – or simply the lure of the unknown. After all, you're a seasoned walker – so why stick to the path?

But before you go off-trail (or bushwhacking, as it's also known), there are some things you should know. Pathways are there for protection: not only to safeguard you from any hidden hazards, but to shelter the flora and fauna too. With your hiking boots and backpack, you're akin to a bulldozer – ploughing through habitats, destroying nests, startling animals and snapping fragile plants. It's also easier to get lost (do you have an OS map with you – and a compass too?) – and you're far more likely to injure yourself on that uneven, unfamiliar terrain. Then, when you're deep in the wilderness, with no phone signal or passers-by, how will you raise the alarm? How will the emergency services find you? Going off-trail is never worth the risk.

70 *Don't... be miserly*

Whether for taxi rides, trinkets or takeout coffee, travellers are generally charged more than locals: not only because you're perceived to be wealthy (and, relatively speaking, you probably are), but tourism is an increasingly rickety business. It can wobble at any moment – we're looking at you, 2020 – so charging a premium in popular areas helps to mitigate that risk.

But you're also not a cash cow. So do your research before you travel: what should you be expecting to shell out for a beer/room/guide? Ask around: what have other travellers paid? And, where possible, do as the locals do: are they travelling around Bangkok by pricey tuk-tuk, or using GrabHitch (a lift-sharing app) instead?

WHAT'S IT WORTH?

If you really can't stomach paying a "tourist tax", then step off the beaten path – even just a little. You'll be amazed at how prices plummet. For example, an espresso in Piazza San Marco, Venice, can cost €15–20 – around 10 times the price you'd be charged a few blocks away.

71 *Don't... take **animal** selfies*

Roger Federer took one with a quokka, Kim Kardashian with an elephant, and Taylor Swift with a kangaroo – and thousands of tourists follow in their footsteps. But why, oh why, are humans so obsessed with taking selfies with animals? It's a trend that worries conservationists and wildlife experts all over the world – especially as (according to research by World Animal Protection) it's becoming increasingly prolific.

Aside from the obvious dangers, such as disrupting wildlife and putting yourself in harm's way, sharing the snaps on social media encourages others to do the same. So even if yours was taken from a distance, with the animal in its natural habitat and you grinning in the foreground, does it really promote a positive wildlife interaction?

"The trouble with wildlife selfies is they often appear without any context. Even if the message is promoting conservation, all people see is someone hugging a penguin – and then they want to do that too."

Professor Philip Seddon, wildlife management expert at New Zealand's Otago University

72

*Don't... add to the plastic **problem***

It's not only plastic bags and bottles that wreak havoc on the environment: it's single-use cutlery, tiny toiletry bottles, disposable cups and so much more – all of which we're far more likely to encounter (and throw away) when we're abroad. So, don't forget to pack your reusable essentials wherever you venture – as well as some biodegradable bubbles for washing them.

Hearteningly, a growing number of countries are clamping down on single-use plastic. Bangladesh was one of the first to address the problem, outlawing plastic bags back in 2002 after litter was linked to heightened flood risk. In 2016, Antigua became the first Caribbean country to banish polythene bags, and then styrofoam packaging – leading the way for many of its island neighbours. In January 2020, China announced it would prohibit non-biodegradable bags in all major cities and towns, while Germany has pledged to stop all sales of single-use plastic by July 2021. Don't be the one that's left behind...

73

*Don't... **dodge** national park fees*

Whether funded by taxation, donations or tourism levies, national parks have to find a way to make money. They have staff to pay, maintenance to do, facilities to manage – and the yearly bill is eye-watering. England's Peak District National Park, for example, costs around £7 million per year to keep open – while the US's National Park Service risks privatization in order to pay for its $12 billion maintenance deficit.

But, all too often, travellers brag about how they've avoided paying any fees, be it for parking, entrance, camping or camera permits. It's seen as a triumph to circumvent shelling out – despite enjoying all the perks that a paying customer would. How blatantly irresponsible is that? *Source: nationalparks.uk*

A SMALL PRICE TO PAY

If you're planning to visit more than one US national park on your holiday, sign up for a Park Pass. At $80 per vehicle/group, you'll get a year of unlimited access to over 2,000 nationwide parks and recreation sites (entry to Yosemite, for example, usually costs $35 per vehicle). It's a win – for both you and the parks (usparkpass.com).

74

Don't... just mix with other tourists

No matter how spectacular your surroundings are, it's often the people that make the place special – be it an incredible guide, a wonderful waiter or a homestay host that treats you like one of the family. So, don't be shy: if you only hang out with your travel buddies, you miss out on so many fleeting connections, or friendships that could last a lifetime.

75 *Don't... drive **off** road*

Tempted to leave the track behind? It's only acceptable if you're...

...with an expert
Someone who has specialist training and knows the terrain like the back of their hand. Let them take the wheel – or give you one-to-one guidance on how to do it right.

...in the right vehicle
Just as you wouldn't climb a mountain in stilettos, don't drive off-piste if your car can't cope with the task. Also, is it – and you – insured?

...at the right place
Off-road driving can destroy the environment: churning up soil, killing plants, clogging up waterways – and much more. If you must do it, head to a purpose-built track.

76

Don't... bring your packaging

You've treated yourself to lots of new gear, clothes and gadgets for this trip – all fresh, new, and still in their packaging. But wait! Where will you dispose of all those tags and boxes? Is there a decent recycling system where you're headed? If not, they could end up in landfill – whereas if you ditched them at home, they'd definitely be recycled. You know what to do...

77 Don't... *flush your wet wipes*

Going camping or long-distance trekking? Choose your wet wipes wisely: Aquaint's Happy Planet Wipes (aquaint-uk.com) are 100 per cent biodegradable and plastic-free. That said, you should always dispose of them responsibly – in a proper bin, and never (ever!) flushed down the toilet.

For menstrual hygiene, a Mooncup (mooncup.co.uk) is a more environmentally friendly choice than tampons or towels, but you'll need to take care when cleaning it. If you don't have access to drinking-quality tap water, you should wash it in treated or filtered water instead. And how will you sterilize it between uses? Think about the practicalities, as well as the environmental cost: ultimately, the choice has to be right for your body.

78

Don't... *trash the trail*

Next time you're hiking or biking, do some litter picking
as you go. It's an easy way to do your bit, and helps to spread
awareness in destinations that aren't so hot on environmental issues.
Thanks to social media campaigns such as #2minutebeachclean and
#binit4beaches, people are hitting the beach with the same attitude:
"Finally, beach cleaning is cool," says the Marine Conservation Society,
"We've waited 25 years for this moment!"

79

Don't... *go jet skiing*

They may look fast and fun, but jet skis wreak indiscriminate havoc
on the environment. They disturb not only marine life but also birds
and land-based animals – and their two-stroke engines (common in
older models) are notorious polluters too. In Florida and Australia, jet
skis and fast-moving watercraft have even been linked to deaths of
manatees and dolphins. Try a snorkelling trip or ocean safari instead.

80 *Don't... forget to smile*

It's easy, it's free and it'll take you far: the power of a smile knows no bounds. We're all taught to keep strangers at arm's length, especially when venturing to far-flung places – but the more you travel, the more you realize that's ridiculous. If you treat everyone as a potential threat, they'll probably do the same to you – or at least think you're just plain strange.

And while, obviously, caution and common sense are essential travelling companions, a big grin can be your (metaphorical) Get Out Of Jail Free card – whether you're haggling in Marrakech, lost in Abu Dhabi or separated from your tour group in the backstreets of Kolkata. Barriers can be broken with just one beam; being stand-offish, meanwhile, will get you nowhere.

Chapter 5
WHAT TO DO

Follow this expert advice to become a superhero of sustainable travel – leaving fantastic things in your wake. How can you give back on your holiday? What should you support? What should you steer clear of? If you try these tips, everyone wins: people, landscapes, wildlife, and you!

81 *Do... respect **local** people*

Just as you'll never forget the people you meet on your travels, they will probably remember you too – so make sure it's for all the right reasons.

Some local customs might jar with your own, but that doesn't mean you shouldn't respect them – at least outwardly. Be it hunting, arranged marriage or the worship of something you deem ridiculous, the world is full of conflicting priorities and ideas. If the local status quo doesn't match yours, make it your mission to learn more about it and to understand why it exists.

In the right context, there's usually no harm in sharing your own views (in a non-confrontational way), but be cautious of offending your hosts and starting battles you can't win. Some people might want to lure you into a heated discussion or try to change your mind, but it's best to politely decline.

82 *Do... give wisely*

When you're approached by street kids asking for money, sweets or pens, it feels heartless not to give them a token or two – after all, what harm could it do? But for all your good intentions, you are probably exacerbating the problem. Many children are actually recruited by exploitative adults and begging gangs to hang around tourism hotspots – and forced to turn over any profits or goods they receive.

Though saying no can feel brutal, it's far better to donate money to a local charity. Alternatively, contact a school or NGO to ask if you can buy some supplies for the kids. Also, consider supporting an international children's charity when you return home – such as Save the Children (savethechildren.org.uk), Unicef (unicef.org.uk) or Street Child (street-child.co.uk).

83

Do... buy *sustainable* souvenirs

Think twice before buying that seashell trinket or feather earrings. You might surmise that the environmental damage has already been done, but by buying the product you're encouraging the vendor to source more.

SHOP SMARTER

- When you're browsing, ask what the goods are made from: sometimes it's obvious (such as fur, bone or shell), but rare woods, animal horn and coral can be harder to spot. Many shopkeepers are proud to sell animal products because they're more expensive than imitations: as such, they're unlikely to keep its gruesome provenance quiet.

- It's amazing what some vendors will try to sell to tourists – and, in many cases, succeed. Bear claws, sharks' teeth, stuffed birds of paradise... If you see something dodgy on show, move along quickly. If you're going to complain to the authorities, you might want to take a photo as evidence – but do so discreetly. Otherwise, some shopkeepers could see their grisly wares as a tourist attraction or get angry at you for taking pictures.

84

Do... go wildlife watching

The emphasis is on *watching* – not petting, posing or stalking. By spending your money on responsible encounters, you're encouraging people to see the value of nurturing wildlife. That's especially vital in places where poaching and illegal trading are rife – such as southern Africa (elephant tusk, rhino horn) and Southeast Asia (turtle shells, pangolin scales). When done correctly, wildlife tourism can create a sustainable local industry that benefits everyone – just take a look at these conservation success stories:

Black rhinos
In 1995, there were just 2,410 black rhinos in Africa – but, thanks to persistent conservation programmes and funding from the safari industry, their numbers have more than doubled.

Blue iguanas
Endemic to the Cayman Islands, these lizards totalled less than a dozen in captivity in the 1990s. Now, there are around 1,000 in Grand Cayman's reserves, and it's the country's national animal.

Humpback whales
By the mid-1950s, humpbacks were threatened by whaling: only an estimated 440 remained in the south Atlantic Ocean. Today there are 25,000, which has created countless tourism jobs.
Sources: savetherhino.org; iucn.org; royalsocietypublishing.org

85

*Do... see dolphins at their **wildest***

For most modern travellers, visiting an aquarium or zoo to see performing dolphins is unthinkable – but that's far from the only way that they are mistreated. Stay away from anywhere that promises dolphin encounters (no matter how wild the location sounds): chances are, they are lured there by feeding – often by hand – which disrupts their natural behaviour, provokes the spread of diseases and encourages harmful interactions with humans.

  Instead, choose a dolphin-watching tour with proven ethical expertise (such as accreditation from the World Cetacean Alliance): their skippers can find dolphins without endangering or spooking them.

86

*Do... be **savvy** about sea life*

Dolphins aren't the only marine animals that are exploited in non-obvious ways. Avoid any shark encounters where interaction is guaranteed: they're likely attracted by chumming, a widely used but often illegal way of attracting sharks by throwing dead fish into the water. Also, stay away from "stingray cities" (in the likes of Antigua and the Cayman Islands), which coax stingrays to sandbars for tourists to hand-feed and hug. These tourist attractions are increasingly popular, and it can be tempting to go along with the crowd – but think twice.

87 *Do... embrace local **cultures***

All over the world, traditions and customs are being eroded. People are shunning their roots in favour of city fortunes, and allowing their native languages to die. But by immersing yourself in these endangered cultures, you'll show how priceless they are. These community-focused tour companies are leading the way – so seek them out, or find others like them:

Tao Philippines
The Palawan archipelago is renowned for its paradise islands – but as luxury hotels have moved in, local people have lost touch with their seafaring traditions. Tao aims to change that, by collaborating with them on sustainable island-hopping adventures: taophilippines.com

Orou Sapulot, Borneo
Once fearsome headhunters, the Murut tribe is now under threat from migration and exploitation. But, by introducing responsible tourism to the tribal area, this enterprising company has empowered local people to protect their culture: orousapulot.com

Discover Aboriginal Experiences, Australia
This collection of tours and activities puts you in touch with Aboriginal guides all over Australia, for a meaningful and immersive experience. Themes include indigenous art, hiking, outback adventure and foodie escapes – with the people who know the land best: australia.com

88

Do... donate unwanted clothes

We've all been there: as your suitcase fills up with souvenirs, you find yourself jettisoning toiletries, shoes and books to make room. But instead of simply throwing them away, try to give them a good home instead: ask the hotel concierge if there's a local charity shop that would welcome a clothing donation, or see if there's a communal bookshelf in your hostel.

In developing countries or deprived areas, your accommodation staff might appreciate any unwanted items – but don't just chuck things in the bin for them to find. Fold up the clothes, dry off shampoo bottles, and try to scrape off any dirt from shoes. Arrange them in a pile, and leave for housekeeping to discover, maybe even with a note to say: "Help yourselves".

89 *Do... learn the language*

English-speakers are notorious for not learning other languages – but is our reputation deserved? Unfortunately, it is. According to a survey by the European Commission, 62 per cent of Britons speak only their mother tongue – meaning that just 38 per cent of us can converse in a foreign language. If you speak three or more different languages, congratulations: you're among only 6 per cent of the population that can do so.

It's a bit embarrassing, isn't it? Especially when you consider that there are around 6,500 languages spoken around the world. Try bucking the trend, then, by learning a few words before you travel – and using them. Don't be shy! Online course providers include Babbel (babbel.com), Duolingo (duolingo.com) and Busuu (busuu.com) – with interactive dialogues, bitesize lessons and phraseology to suit modern life.

Load up your phone with a translation app, too: the likes of Google Translate and iTranslate offer offline functionality for multiple languages, so you can communicate clearly wherever you are.

90 *Do... honour your promises*

Be honest: how many times have you promised to keep in touch with someone, then never got around to doing it? We all make pledges that, in the moment, feel right and simple – you've connected to a person or place, so why wouldn't you want to keep communicating when you're home? But real life gets in the way – and before you know it, you've forgotten to transfer that photo, upload that review or write that email you vowed to send.

Instead, take the first step while you're travelling home. Put your return flight or train journey to good use by drafting your first communication: not only will the details be fresh in your mind, but if you've already begun your conversation you'll find continuing it easier when you're back in "real life". Embrace social media, too: if you're happy to add someone to your network, ask if they'd like to stay connected that way.

91 *Do... tip responsibly*

Before you travel, check whether tipping is customary – and how much, for whom and in which contexts. It doesn't matter whether you agree with tipping or not, or whether it's part of your own culture: for many people around the world, tips are the only way to supplement a meagre income.

Of course, expectations vary wildly by destination. In Mexico, for example, a tip (or *propina*) of 10–15 per cent in restaurants is customary, while in Indonesia a 10 per cent service charge is usually added automatically to the bill – with some diners choosing to give a little extra, too. However, in some areas of Asia – including Japan, South Korea and China – tipping can be seen as an insult. If in doubt, ask a local person or make a discreet enquiry at your hotel.

DON'T FORGET YOUR GUIDE!
Just like waiters, drivers and porters, many guides rely on customer tips – even those employed by international tour operators. Make sure you check your trip notes for guidance, and always hand over money discreetly: pack an envelope to put it in, and maybe even a "thank you" card too.

92 *Do... clean your boots*

Just as you wouldn't hide non-native plant seeds or insect eggs in your luggage, make sure you're not transporting them on your clothes or shoes either.

It's especially important on hiking trips. At Australia's Kosciuszko National Park – home to the country's highest peak – researchers found that walkers were inadvertently spreading invasive plant species as they explored the area. During just one hiking season, an estimated 1.9 million seeds were being carried on visitors' socks, while 2.4 million were transported on trousers – and some were still attached at the end of a five-kilometre (three-mile) walk.

DID YOU KNOW?

On arrival in New Zealand, you'll be asked to declare any hiking boots, camping equipment or sports gear at customs. If it's not clean, it may be confiscated and destroyed.

93

Do... ask *permission* before taking photos

Always ask before taking someone's photo, but use discretion if pushed for payment: it can encourage begging and exploitation. It's better to purchase a souvenir or service, and then ask the vendor if it's alright to snap a few shots.

If you're tempted to capture an impromptu portrait, ask yourself how you'd feel if the tables were turned. As any photographer will tell you, the best snaps come with colourful backstories – a tale to tell about the person or place that it features. So get to know your subject a little: strike up a conversation, buy something or at least give them a smile. Even if there's a language barrier, a simple point to your camera and an "OK?" will usually suffice – and if they say no, don't push it.

94 *Do... set an* ***example***

If you see someone doing something that isn't right, it's not always wise to confront them. Of course, in the right context it's perfectly acceptable – but if it's not, remember that actions speak louder than words. Do the right thing, and hope that they see you and follow your lead. Sometimes, that's the best you can do.

95 *Do... spread* *your* ***money***

How far does your cash actually go? If you favour cruise holidays, package trips and all-inclusive resorts, your entire holiday budget might go to just one company – and that's fine, as long as it's a good one. They, in turn, will support other businesses and hopefully charities too.

It's usually far better, however, to support lots of independent enterprises – especially while you're away. And don't be a sheep! Everyone else might flock to the obvious restaurants, hotels and attractions – but you don't have to. Find somewhere different instead.

96

*Do... share **great** experiences*

It's tempting to keep a "hidden gem" to yourself: to stay quiet about that amazing restaurant, homestay or city tour. After all, it was fantastic because it was so crowd-free and authentic, right? If it shot to fame, it would lose all appeal – don't you think? Well, try explaining that to your hosts...

Without guest recommendations and glowing reviews, many tourism businesses simply wouldn't survive. And as much as you enjoyed having the place/tour/attraction all to yourself, it might not last long if you don't support it now. You have to trust that its proprietor has a plan to manage its growth sustainably – and wouldn't it be great to play your part in the expansion of an independent business or local entrepreneur? If you return one day, you might explain to them that you were one of the first customers – and helped to spread the word afterwards. That would be a far bigger buzz than keeping those travel tips all to yourself.

97

*Do... report those who **aren't** doing their bit*

If you think your tour operator or hotel could operate in a
more responsible way, say so. Make your thoughts clear in a
review, in person, or send an email to management – and, in
extreme cases, contact the tourist board or travel trade body
ABTA (abta.com) for advice.

Were there any moments in your trip where you felt
uncomfortable? Did the itinerary include hotels that
weren't managed sustainably? Most tour operators
provide hundreds of different holidays, and rely on
feedback to ensure their partners are acting
responsibly. If they're not, it's your duty
to speak up.

98 *Do... **champion** those who are*

Think your hotel/guide/tour operator went the extra mile? Shout about it! Use social media, review sites and feedback channels to spread the word. It's great encouragement for businesses to do better and lets fellow travellers know who's championing ethical and responsible practices. If we're going to make travel even more sustainable, we need to keep the conversation going – and support the enterprises and people who are already doing their bit.

99 *Do... **forgive** yourself*

Even the most responsible traveller has done things they're not proud of. In less enlightened times you might have posed with a lion, enjoyed a dune-bashing trip or pocketed souvenir shells from the beach. But don't carry the guilt around with you, berating yourself for being naive. Instead, make it your mission to travel better in future. If you can't forgive and forget, try:

- Donating or volunteering for charity. Find one that rights the wrongs you might have unwittingly made over the years.

- Carbon offsetting all those long-haul minibreaks and frivolous trips. It won't fix the problem, but it can help.

- Owning up to your mistakes. It takes guts to admit you were wrong in the past, but telling others will help spread awareness.

100

Do...
*be **kind***

Wherever you venture, you'll leave a lasting impression – so make sure it's the right one. Can you look back on your trip with pride and integrity? Did it leave a positive impact on people and places? If so, bravo. Hold your head up high! The world needs more travellers like you.

Resources

FURTHER READING

Only Planet: A Flight-Free Adventure Around the World (Ed Gillespie)
Ed is on a mission to circumnavigate the Earth without setting foot on
a plane – a high-spirited tale of cargo ships, camels and more...

Overbooked: The Exploding Business of Travel and Tourism (Elizabeth
Becker)
How sustainable is the tourism industry? Elizabeth shines a light on
the issues that matter most.

Wanderlust magazine (wanderlust.co.uk)
The bible for all adventurous travellers, with eco-friendly and
conscious travel at its heart. Available in print and online.

The Journal (intrepidtravel.com/adventures)
Curated by Intrepid Travel, this responsible adventure blog is
informative and inspirational.

WEBSITES

greenfins.net
A must-read for scuba divers, with listings for responsible dive centres
and liveaboards around the world.

worldanimalprotection.org
*Champions of conservation, WAP curates global wildlife news, travel
tips and documentaries.*

seat61.com
A one-stop-shop for train travel tips, helping you plot long-distant and low-impact routes. See also greentraveller.co.uk.

DOCUMENTARIES
Blackfish (2013)
A heart-wrenching look behind the scenes of the sea-park industry, and its mistreatment of killer whales.

Chasing Coral (2017)
A team of scientists, divers and photographers document the disappearance of the world's coral reefs.

PODCASTS
Flight Free (flightfree.co.uk)
Interviews with scientists, campaigners and travellers who've pledged to stop flying – but not stop exploring.

Overheard at National Geographic (nationalgeographic.com/podcasts/overheard)
Conversations with some of Nat Geo's top writers, and the stories they've covered – such as wildlife trafficking and remote conservation.

The Thoughtful Travel Podcast (Apple Podcasts)
Hosted by Amanda Kendle, this indie podcast delves into responsible travel issues – with a chatty and informative style.

Websites

Index
